P9-CAD-187

YUSRA SWIMS

Julie Abery
illustrated by Sally Deng

Creative Editions

Just a girl
With a dream.
Olympic Games
Swimming team.

Unrest spreads,
Conflict strains.
Staying focused,
Yusra trains.

Hometown siege,
People flee.

War-torn country,
Refugee.

Say farewell.
Tears goodbye.

Parting under
Hostile sky.

Foreign square,
Smugglers paid.
Filling buses,
Nerves are frayed.

Camping out,
Friendships grow,

Waiting for their
Time to go.

Crowded boat,
Fading light,
Slipping quickly
Out of sight.

Open sea,
Cold and wet.
Overflowing,
Not safe yet.

Engine fails,
Sinking boat.
Throw possessions,
Stay afloat.

Treading water,
Gripping rope.
Yusra swims,
Keeping hope.

Water deep.
Crashing waves.
Pushing forward,
Being brave.

Cold and numb,
Faces gray.
Final landing,
Fall and pray.

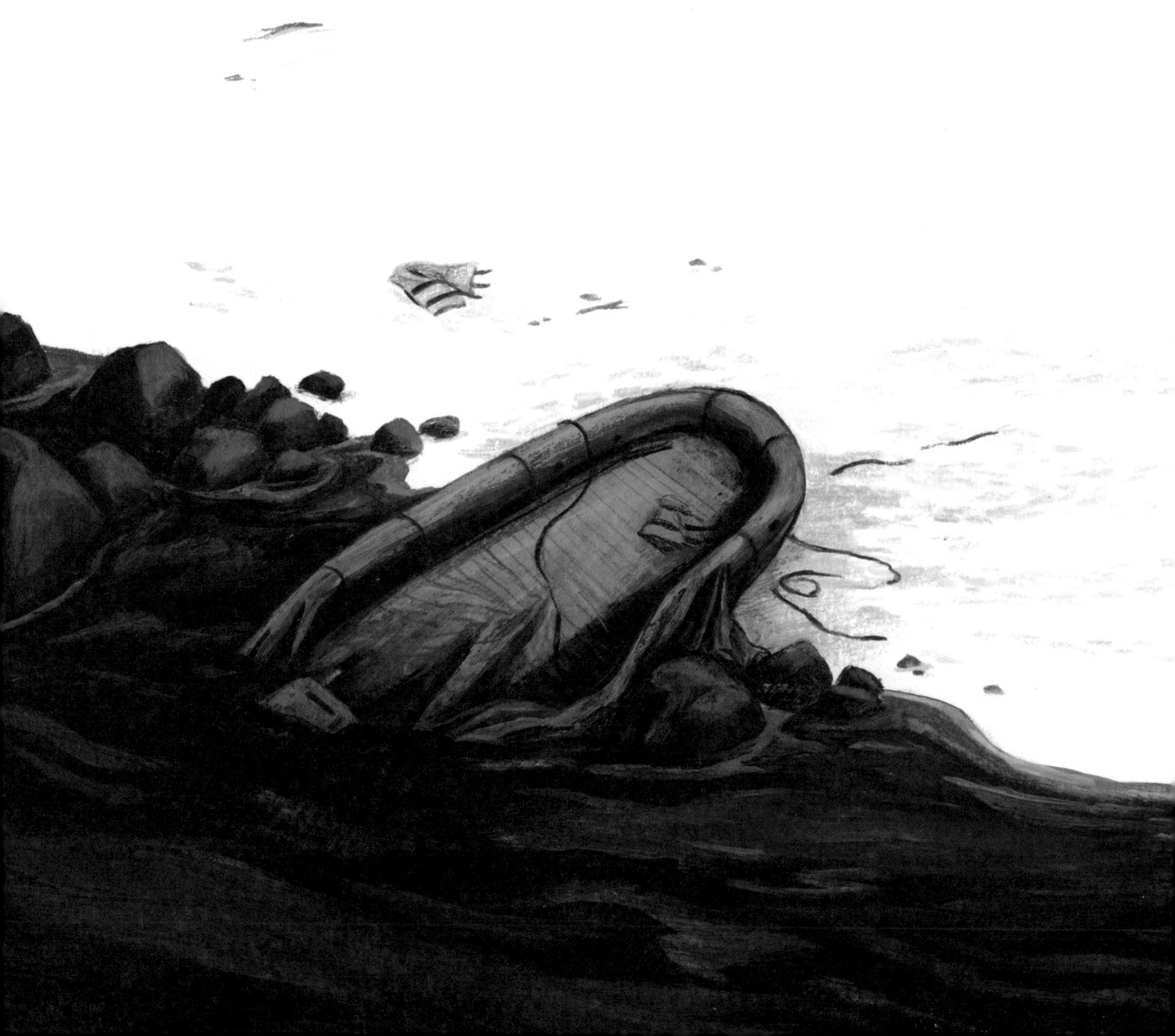

Strangers stare,
Looks accuse.

Sudden kindness,
Given shoes.

Miles to go,
Rough terrain.
Trekking, buses,
Then by train.

Safe at last.
End of line.
Smiling faces.
Welcome sign.

New hometown,
House, and school.
Training daily
In the pool.

Refugee
Olympic team.
Yusra swims.
Achieves her dream.

ABOUT YUSRA MARDINI

Yusra Mardini grew up in Damascus, Syria, where she trained as a competitive swimmer. She represented her country in the 2012 FINA World Swimming Championships. But in the summer of 2015, the Syrian Civil War began to escalate all around. Yusra and her family had lost their home and moved several times to avoid the worsening conflict, but when a bomb burst through the roof of the swimming complex and fell into the pool where she was training, she knew that she had to leave Syria.

Leaving would be fraught with danger and also expensive. Yusra's father researched the journey and provided the money to pay for 17-year-old Yusra and her older sister to flee to Europe. The two sisters flew to Istanbul, Turkey. They traveled by bus to the Turkish coast, where they boarded a dinghy bound for the Greek island of Lesbos. Fifteen minutes into the journey, the boat's engine failed, and it began to take on water. The Mardini sisters and two other passengers bravely jumped into the sea; it took them three and a half hours to safely guide the boat to shore.

From Lesbos, Yusra continued her journey by ferry and foot, by road and train, traveling through Greece, Macedonia, Serbia, Hungary, and Austria, all the way to Berlin, Germany. Twenty-five days later, she and her sister settled in Berlin. The Mardinis were eventually reunited in their new home just before Christmas.

Yusra joined a competitive swim club, where her new swim coach trained her back into top condition. In 2016, she was among 10 athletes invited by the International Olympic Committee to participate in the Rio de Janeiro Olympics as part of the Refugee Olympic Team. As the story of Yusra's incredible journey spread, she soon became a vocal advocate for the plight of refugees. In 2017, she was appointed a United Nations High Commissioner for Refugees (UNHCR*) Goodwill Ambassador.

*UNHCR, also known as the UN Refugee Agency, is a global organization dedicated to saving lives, protecting rights, and building a better future for refugees, forcibly displaced communities, and stateless people. They lead international action to protect people forced to flee their homes because of conflict and persecution. They work in more than 125 countries, using their expertise to protect and care for nearly 64 million people. www.unhcr.org/yusra-mardini

 Edited by Amy Novesky; designed by Rita Marshall Published in 2020 by Creative Editions P.O. Box 227, Mankato, MN 56002 USA Creative Editions is an imprint of The Creative Company www.thecreativecompany.us Printed in China
Library of Congress Cataloging-in-Publication Data Names: Abery, Julie, author. / Deng, Sally, illustrator. Title: Yusra swims / by Julie Abery; illustrated by Sally Deng. Summary: A biography in rhyme relates the story of Olympic swimmer and Syrian refugee Yusra Mardini. Identifiers: LCCN 2019029595 / ISBN 978-1-56846-329-2 Subjects: LCSH: Mardini, Yusra—Juvenile literature. / Swimmers—Syria—Biography—Juvenile literature. / Olympic athletes—Syria —Biography—Juvenile literature. / Refugees—Syria—Biography—Juvenile literature. Classification: LCC GV838.M366 A24 2020 / DDC 797.2/1092 [B]—dc23 First edition 9 8 7 6 5 4 3 2 1